UNLOCKING THE CODE

Deciphering IRS Negotiations with Easily Understood Analogy and Real-World Examples from the Trenches

Steve Cizik, Esq.

Jacobs & Whitehall
9600 Escarpment Blvd
Suite 745-282
Austin, TX 78749
www.jacobsandwhitehall.com

Ordering Information:

Quantity sales. Special discounts are available on quantity purchases by corporations, associations, and others. For details, contact the publisher at the address above.

Orders by U.S. trade bookstores and wholesalers. Please contact Jacobs & Whitehall: Tel: (888) 570-7338 or visit www.jacobsandwhitehall.com.

Printed in the United States of America

Published in 2024

PREFACE

As a young lawyer with my first child (a boy) on the way, I felt it a grand gesture to purchase a hardback copy of "A Dangerous Book for Boys" by Gonn and Hal Iggulden and write something on the inside cover that would carry weight. Understanding that I was flirting with being entirely sappy and a bit contrived, I wrote the following, "Knowledge is power. Be AWESOME. Love, Dad". Nearly a decade and a half later, I've found that those words still ring true both professionally and personally. If this book brings that knowledge and requisite power to even one individual or business owner who read it . . . we'll have had a great success.

Dedication

For the countless staff and support members, namely Brandy, Amanda, Abrianna, Kyle, George, Evalina, Sarah, Jackie and above all Victoria - without your tireless assistance, patience, and dedication to our Team and clients, none of our success would have been possible.

DISCLAIMER

This publication is intended to be used for educational purposes only. No legal advice is being given, and no attorney-client relationship is intended to be created by reading this material. The author assumes no liability for any errors or omissions or for how this book or its contents are used or interpreted, or for any consequences resulting directly or indirectly from the use of this book. For legal or any other advice, please consult an experienced attorney or the appropriate expert, who is aware of the specific facts of your case and is knowledgeable in the law in your jurisdiction.

The Harris Law Firm,
Complex Tax Law Division
1125 17th Street, Suite 450
Denver, CO 80202
complextaxlaw.com
303.720.6573
303.515.5015

TESTIMONIALS

"Working with Steve Cizik has been one of the best investments we have made as a family, and he has personally managed a wide range of complex business, personal, and estate tax matters for us. Steve and his team are exceptional and professional at every step, going above and beyond in ways no other law firms or professionals have done for us before. It is rare to find someone who is as honest and capable as Steve. He listens to your needs and is able to provide thoughtful, effective answers and strategies. He has extensive experience dealing with complex issues and has accomplished more for us in months than previous firms have done in years. Highly recommend."

– DD

****

"Steve consulted with me about a vacation rental taxation issue and gave me some very helpful advice. He is a very kind and thoughtful person. I hope to not need his services again, but if I do I'd be delighted to work with him."

– Nathaniel Farber

****

"Steve has been a wealth of great knowledge for my clients needing advice on various tax issues and the IRS. Call him before you try to handle anything with the IRS on your own!"

— Joe DiSanto

****

"Steve is very thorough and tactical with his approach. He was brought into every complex case with a very short timeline and more than exceeded expectations. I would highly recommend him for any forensic accounting work."

— Chad Huggins

****

"Steve is a very honest attorney. He provided me with so much information on how I may be able to fix my situation without his help, at no charge. He took the time to help out a mama in desperate need. I highly recommend Steve."

— Arlette Jervis

****

TABLE OF CONTENTS

i.	Preface	3
ii.	Dedication	4
iii.	Disclaimer	5
iv.	Testimonials	6
v.	About The Author	10
1.	Brain Damage & Intellectual Backflips: My Approach To The Intricacies Of IRS Negotiations	15
2.	Lollipops And Hummingbirds: Penalties & Interest	23
3.	Killing Trees: The "Impact" Of IRS Notices	30
4.	Institutional Inefficiency: The IRS Collections Process	39
5.	The Truth Will Set You Free: Navigating Financial Production & Analysis	45

6. Help Me Help You: Agreements & Offers 51

7. That Just Got Spicy: Levies, Seizures, & Garnishments 60

8. A Second Bite At The Apple: The Power Of Appeals 65

9. Kid Gloves: Handling Tax Liens With Care 71

10. The Buck Stops With You: The Truth About Trust Fund Assessments 76

11. Putting Lipstick On A Pig: Successor & Alter Ego Determinations 82

12. Tap Dancing On The Head Of The Needle: Navigating Audits & Reconsiderations 90

13. Knowledge Is Power: The World Of Forensic Auditing 96

14. Something Fishy Is Going On: Expert Testimony & Personal Experiences 102

vi. Index 109

vii. Notes 111

About The Author

My Journey Into The World Of Tax Law

I'm Steve Cizik, and my relationship with tax law has represented an intellectual and emotional tour de force over almost 15 years. As a native of Colorado educated at CU Boulder, my journey took an unexpected turn following multiple career-ending knee surgeries during my time on the CU Freestyle Ski Team. Subsequently, the need to refocus both my energy and competitive drive led me to Syracuse Law School, where I graduated cum laude. Upon my return to Denver, my career took off, first with three years in complex corporate litigation where I found my skill set suited for specializing in financial cases. Over time, my career (somewhat unnaturally) veered into tax representation – a field that I never anticipated would culminate in an incredibly rewarding career path that I have stuck with ever since.

Six years ago, Complex Tax Law Firm was born, and I would ultimately join the Harris Law Firm heading its Tax Division with a sturdy focus on complex taxation, compliance and conflict cases. We primarily aid companies grappling with payroll and income tax issues, ensuring their business wheels keep turning even in trying times. Our expertise also extends to intricate taxation matters, corporate restructuring, and providing expert advice and testimony in various disputes, both in and out of the taxation context.

Entertaining Encounters In Tax Law

Believe it or not, being a tax attorney can be quite entertaining. The thrill emanates from dealing with a medley of people, emotions, and high-stakes situations, particularly involving businesses and crucial financial moments. The unique personalities of clients who find themselves under the IRS's microscope, either due to inadvertent oversights or deliberate actions, bring about myriad stories and experiences. This book aims to not only be informative but also provide a smattering of entertainment through stories from the field, highlighting the sometimes convoluted interactions and negotiations with the IRS.

Despite tax law and accounting often being seen as stringent and "black and white," the legal negotiations involved contain many shades of gray. There is a palpable dichotomy between what the Tax Code dictates and how an IRS representative interprets or is willing to apply that Code during negotiations or appeals. This often turns scenarios into a "laugh or cry" situation, and the book seeks to share these in a light yet educational manner.

Chess With The IRS: An Insightful Battle

Navigating through IRS negotiations, for me, resembles an intricate chess match. Over years and numerous client interactions, I've accumulated knowledge and practical tactics in dealing with the IRS - which at times is seen as a form of voluntary suffering! However, despite the IRS being a dominant and occasionally perplexing entity to work with, I've managed to carve out enjoyable and constructive experiences, ensuring beneficial outcomes for my clients by adopting a strategic, foresighted approach in my dealings with them.

Who Stands To Gain From This Book?

While anyone can find value in these pages, this book particularly speaks to those engulfed in high-stress negotiations or those dealing with clients in critical situations where significant implications loom over every discussion's outcome. Though my experiences derive from IRS negotiations and client dealings, the principles and techniques shared are transcendent, applicable across various contexts of negotiation and dispute resolution.

As such, this book aims not to provide a purely instructional guide on dealing with the IRS but offers a broader perspective, providing a high-altitude view on managing crucial negotiations. So, whether you're a tax attorney, a CPA looking for insights into handling complex issues, or anyone seeking to glean knowledge on navigating high-stakes negotiations, this book aims to assist, inform, and perhaps even entertain a little along the way.

CHAPTER 1

BRAIN DAMAGE & INTELLECTUAL BACKFLIPS: MY APPROACH TO THE INTRICACIES OF IRS NEGOTIATIONS

The Philosophical Foundations Of My Approach To IRS Negotiations

Throughout my career, my interactions with clients have naturally woven into my philosophical approach toward IRS negotiations, stemming directly from my personality and the realities I've witnessed within the complex landscape of tax negotiations. The phrases I employ, such as referencing "brain damage" and performing "intellectual back flips," are not merely artistic flourishes for this book, but real descriptors of the cognitive and strategic efforts I exert when engaging in these negotiations.

My journey into the intricate world of IRS discussions, whether dealing with Revenue Officers, summonses, or other entities, always encompasses an acknowledgment that these paths are never straightforward. My clients appreciate this transparency and the resultant setting of accurate expectations, comprehending that while the process may be time-consuming and intricate, my dedication will unfailingly help them navigate through the complexities they face.

The History Of Negotiation Methodology And Law And Why It Is So Important

Back when I was involved in corporate litigation, particularly in the realm of financial matters, the role of lawyers in finalizing transactions was evident. Whether it's a straightforward contract or a complex merger and acquisition deal, lawyers play a pivotal role in turning a handshake agreement into a legally binding document. The essence of what a lawyer brings to the table lies in the act of putting the terms on paper, ensuring they are well-vetted, and thereby legitimizing the transaction.

Despite the plethora of lawyer jokes and the love-hate relationship people have with them, their presence is indispensable in this process. Negotiation is an integral part of this journey. In many instances, one or more parties involved may not fully comprehend their rights, especially in cases where one party, like the IRS, is represented and the other isn't. This is where a lawyer's negotiation skills come into play: A proficient lawyer can negotiate both efficiently and effectively.

While there are instances where legal counsel may excel in one aspect of the process while faltering in the other, the true value emerges when a lawyer can excel at both, providing comprehensive representation to their client or business. It is counterproductive to burden a business with exorbitant legal fees just to conclude a negotiation. On the other hand, securing a bargain deal that ultimately falls apart is equally detrimental. Thus, the importance of having a lawyer who possesses the prowess to negotiate adeptly, legitimize contracts, elucidate the rationale behind their actions to the client, and present viable options cannot be overstated. Ultimately, the lawyer's role is to leave the client content with the negotiated outcome while offering the assurance that the process was executed correctly.

Exploring The Nuances Of Tax Negotiation

Tax negotiation unveils its uniqueness through the lens of the distinct power dynamics between the taxpayer and the IRS. With the latter often being perceived as almost omnipotent, a tax attorney becomes a critical intermediary, serving as a shield between the taxpayer and the potent authority of IRS officers or Appeals Officers. It is essential that clients feel secure, understanding that they have an advocate in their corner, safeguarding them from the metaphorical lions at the gate. An anecdote from an interaction with a client, a Colorado restaurant owner facing seemingly straightforward tax issues, highlights this effectively. Although the situation might have been resolved without legal intervention, the client firmly underscored the value of having an expert navigate the tax waters, humorously asserting, "I'll cook the chicken, you call the state."

In this realm, tax attorneys often don the cap of a psychologist, offering reassurance and guidance through the taxing process while also ensuring clients don't pay more than the law demands. At times, aiming for a more favorable and intangible outcome than expected becomes the target during negotiations with tax authorities. This is achieved by perpetually upholding the principle of offering peace of mind to clients and ensuring that strategies are transparent and agreed upon.

Navigating Through Different Business Scenarios

A myriad of scenarios exists where businesses might find themselves entwined in tax negotiations.

Taking one case as an example, a client in New York, despite having corporate protections for substantial personal assets, was an Officer an entity that incurred significant tax liability due to running a payroll-intensive business. Once the IRS began to send notices and pursue Collections, the necessity to protect not only the business's accounts, but also that Officer's substantial and now exposed personal assets and income became paramount. Thus, the involvement of an attorney was crucial to confirm a strategy that safeguarded assets while simultaneously stopping the financial "bleeding" and emotional turmoil the client was experiencing personally This entailed ensuring compliance, starting tax payments, and aligning returns, followed by setting up a payment arrangement to prevent the IRS from seizing BOTH personal and business equipment or assets.

Complex scenarios also unfold, such as divorce cases where a spouse may be hiding assets behind numerous entities, requiring a forensic audit to unearth those funds and assist in family law cases. Addressing lien identification is another common task, such as a challenging case where, amidst the tragedy of the recently well publicized Colorado wildfires, a client sought to purchase a new home. Here, the negotiation skills of a tax attorney became pivotal to working with the state and the IRS, ensuring lien releases and verifying the same with the title company and underwriter, thereby allowing individuals to move beyond financial encumbrances.

Negotiating With Pragmatism And Professionalism

In my experience, having grown up in Littleton, Colorado, embarking on a journey to learn the legal practice in Syracuse, New York and then returning back to work and live in Denver, Colorado, the variance in legal negotiation styles became starkly evident. Whereas Syracuse's methodology leaned towards an assertive, "hammer-like" approach, Denver offered a perspective that prioritized pragmatism and forethought in negotiations.

Transitioning from litigation to negotiation, it became evident that approaching IRS agents with a demeanor that is professional, pragmatic, and expecting perfection without aggressive overtones proved to be more effective. Today, I've found that successfully engaging with IRS agents requires you to build a reputation that encourages them to work with you rather than pushes them to avoid interaction due to your bulldog-like reputation.

Revenue Officers, Appeals Officers, group managers, and territory managers have often demonstrated a preference to work with negotiators who employ a non-aggressive, pragmatic methodology over those who adopt a highly aggressive stance. So it's clear: Balancing professionalism with forethought and straightforwardness emerges as a winning formula in IRS negotiations, thus ensuring the attorney protects their client's interests while maintaining a cooperative relationship with tax authorities.

CHAPTER 2

LOLLIPOPS AND HUMMINGBIRDS: PENALTIES & INTEREST

I often liken strategies that promise to remove or abate penalties and interest to "lollipops and hummingbirds." Of course, it would be wonderful if everything in the tax world were as delightful as lollipops and hummingbirds - you could even throw in rainbows and unicorns for good measure. However, that's not the reality.

The IRS isn't in the business of casually waiving penalties or interest when you don't pay on time. In fact, their primary mission is to collect as much money as possible, and that's the core of their ethos and operations. So, when a client approaches and hopes to have all their penalties and interest wiped away, it's important to understand that the IRS is not inclined to do that. You have to keep in mind that these penalties are designed to incentivize everyone to pay their taxes on time and correctly.

Penalty And Interest Abatement Strategies

At times when I am discussing removal of liabilities with clients, I explain that if I had a drawer full of penalty abatements that I could simply send in to get everyone's penalties removed, I'd be retired by now. Unfortunately, it doesn't work that way, but this doesn't mean we can't get penalties removed in some cases, and in certain situations, we can also have some interest removed. Still, there are strategies that allow you to work within the IRS structure to save as much money as possible.

For example, I worked with a client who hadn't filed a return since 2016. We utilized a tax structure where, if you file a return and haven't had tax issues for three years prior, you can include a form with your tax return to request the removal of penalties and interest. We structured it so that he filed one return first, got the penalties removed, and then filed subsequent returns at three-year intervals. By using these **"first-time abatement"** strategies, he ended up saving tens of thousands of dollars in penalties. If we had filed them all at the same time, we would have only qualified for the first-time abatement on one of the returns.

Another option is to submit a **"reasonable cause request"** where you acknowledge your mistake but explain that there were circumstances beyond your control that led to late payments or filings.

I had a client who owned a race car team for an organization who identifies itself with six letters. The tax issues were a result of an unforeseeable problem with one of their car suppliers, which prevented them from racing. When they couldn't race, they couldn't earn money, yet they were still incurring expenses for their racing team. I filed a reasonable cause request for this client arguing that they couldn't have foreseen the situation that prevented them from participating in races and earning substantial income. In the end, we successfully got around $190,000 in penalties removed.

In general, the IRS will consider removing penalties when you can demonstrate that the circumstances were completely out of your control, and you acted as a reasonably prudent business person to fulfill your tax obligations. However, stories like "I had a bad year, so I chose not to pay my taxes" will carry less weight in these situations.

What To Do If You Disagree With Penalties Or Charges

If a business believes that they've been inaccurately assessed penalties or fees, there are avenues for appeal. One option is to file an appeal based on **"doubt as to liability,"** where you challenge the accuracy of the penalties or charges themselves, stating that you don't believe you owe them.

Additionally, if you believe the penalties are justified but you're experiencing financial hardship, you can explore an "Offer in Compromise," which allows you to offer the IRS an amount less than what you owe, based on your financial situation.

Impact Of Penalties And Balances On A Company's Financial Stability

Penalties can be particularly burdensome because they can be significant and often accumulate over time. These penalties can also compound with interest charges, making the total amount owed much larger. As such, it's important for business owners to understand that when they owe the IRS, they typically owe the entire amount, including penalties and interest.

This can have a significant impact on a company's financial stability, as it may lead to cash flow issues and strained resources. However, it's crucial to remember that panicking or shutting down the company is rarely the best solution. The best approach is to look at the situation rationally and work on a plan to address the outstanding liabilities over time.

Relief Options For Businesses Impacted By Natural Disasters Or Economic Downturns

In cases of natural disasters or economic downturns, there are often tax relief options available to those who are impacted. For example, if a business is located in an area affected by a hurricane, wildfire, or another disaster, they may be granted extensions for filing tax returns or paying taxes. This is typically based on proof of the location and the extent of the disaster's impact.

Economic downturns, such as those experienced during the COVID-19 pandemic, have also led to certain relief measures. Many penalties and interest charges related to tax liabilities in these situations have been temporarily waived or reduced. The key is to document how the business was affected and provide supporting evidence when requesting relief.

In summary, while the IRS may not readily remove all penalties and interest charges, there are strategies and relief options available for businesses facing tax issues. It's essential to work with a tax professional who can help navigate these processes and advocate for the best possible outcome.

CHAPTER 3

KILLING TREES: THE "IMPACT" OF IRS NOTICES

The Irony Of The IRS And The Paperwork Reduction Act

In 1998, the IRS introduced the Government Paperwork Elimination Act, a rather ironic name considering the sheer volume of paper notices they generate. Why is it so ironic? Let's consider this scenario: A client of mine has eight years of tax liabilities, which translates to four quarters of withholding for each of those years. We have an installment agreement in place, and if they happen to miss a single payment, we're inundated with four certified notices for each of the eight years of liability. What's more, these notices are sent not only to me and my firm but also to the client. The result? A multitude of paper notifications, all essentially saying the same thing - "You missed a payment." This inefficiency is why I playfully refer to it as "killing trees." The Paperwork Reduction Act, in practice, seems far from its intended purpose, as the volume of notices sent out vastly overshadows their actual relevance to a case.

Sometimes, these notices are nothing more than a scare tactic, designed to prompt a response. To address this, I at one point added a humorous touch to my email signature, featuring a small green leaf and the message, "Thank you for receiving my email. Please print and burn immediately as per the Paperwork Production Act of 1998." Surprisingly, it went unnoticed for five years until one attorney finally appreciated the jab.

Common Reasons Businesses Receive IRS Notices

The reasons behind businesses receiving IRS notices can vary significantly. These notices often fall into two categories: those intended to intimidate or evoke fear and those that hold genuine negotiation implications. The former category includes what we often call "glorified balance due notices," which assert that a significant amount is owed and immediate payment is required, sometimes with the threat of a notice of intent to levy. These notices typically arrive in green envelopes, designed to catch your attention.

However, it's really the seemingly innocuous notices that demand the most attention. They may arrive in plain envelopes, subtly labeled "final notice," but they carry a much more significant impact on the negotiation process. The IRS has a method to their madness when it comes to collections. They employ an aggressive approach initially to grab your attention, but once they progress through the notice phase and can proceed with collections, they become less vocal and less concerned with notices. This shift demands vigilance on the recipient's part to navigate the IRS's ever-changing timeline.

The Myriad Of IRS Notices For Businesses

The IRS issues a multitude of notice types, each identified by a distinct code, such as CP 90, LT 11, or CP 523. Each of these codes can indicate either audit assessments, balance due notices, and various other forms of communication. But while tax professionals may be familiar with these designations, our clients generally are not. Surprisingly, even the IRS occasionally struggles to identify its own notices, requiring clarification during phone calls.

As I've encountered firsthand, the IRS's recent influx of new employees has sometimes resulted in training that's outright lacking. During one phone call, I had to fax the notice to the person on the other end - even indicating where to find the most basic information - to prevent a proposed assessment of over a million dollars. It's astonishing how someone's inability to perform a simple task, such as clicking a button on a computer, can have such a significant impact.

Of course, that's why so many people choose to work with a lawyer on these matters. The role of a tax attorney often entails identifying issues, devising solutions, and communicating effectively with the IRS to rectify the situation. This means that if the IRS representative lacks knowledge, you're not stuck in a position where you can't find a resolution for your case. Instead, your attorney will work to determine the appropriate steps to resolve the matter - even if that means guiding the IRS through it themselves.

Responding To IRS Notices: Timelines And Complexities

IRS notices typically assert that you must respond within 30 days of the notice date, but this can vary significantly depending on the notice type. For example, some notices afford a mere 15-day response window, while others suggest 60 or 90 days. What's more, the advertised response time can actually be misleading, often serving as a mere suggestion. But that doesn't mean that you should procrastinate, waiting around for the issue to resolve itself. Failing to act promptly can result in missed opportunities, such as missing the statute of limitations for refund claims.

The reality is that navigating these timelines demands an in-depth understanding of IRS procedures – because the IRS deliberately crafts a complex web, sometimes causing taxpayers to surrender or make errors that lead to the collection process. As such, reading the full notice is crucial, and if it seems perplexing, seeking guidance from a professional who comprehends the intricacies of the tax code and IRS processes is definitely in your best interest.

Options For Businesses Disputing IRS Notices

Businesses have various options when disputing the information or claims presented in IRS notices. While some cases may seem hopeless, avenues for resolution do exist. Procedural stop-gaps, Advocate requests, and multiple layers of Appeals are available

In many instances, the IRS will issue penalties, sometimes even substantial ones, due to seemingly trivial issues. For example, if the IRS fails to receive a company's W2 forms that were correctly filed with the Social Security Administration, they may impose significant penalties. A certified public accountant (CPA) might include the missing W2s with a letter and send them to the IRS, but these forms may languish for years before being processed. Meanwhile, the company accrues substantial Tax Liens, assessments or penalties that should never have been assessed. Navigating these negotiations requires a strategic approach, ensuring that the correct paperwork reaches the right hands.

Fortunately, situations like these are exactly where firms like ours step in. At Complex Tax Law Division, we play a crucial role in helping businesses understand and respond effectively to IRS notices and letters. In fact, sometimes just knowing how to address an issue is more critical than being "right" in the eyes of the IRS. Merely insisting that you're right without navigating the bureaucratic process correctly can lead to frustration. In the worst cases, it can cause people to settle for a situation that doesn't reflect their rights or best interests. Our goal is to prevent you from reaching this point.

For example, consider this situation: A client approached us with a staggering $600,000 in tax liability stemming from a case he had actually won against the IRS in tax court. Unfortunately, his prior attorney failed to file a critical document, resulting in personal assessments and the threat of potential actions against him and his wife. Meanwhile, his CPA and previous attorney had sent countless letters to the wrong IRS processing unit, accomplishing little. Within a month, we realized that their argument was strong but directed at the wrong place. We needed to engage the right individuals and follow a different path. It took nearly a decade, but we successfully resolved the issue, reducing his payment from $600,000 to a mere $6,000. Of course, this outcome could have been avoided entirely if he had sought our assistance a decade earlier.

In summary, reaching out to our firm before problems escalate can save substantial time, effort, and stress. However, if a business finds itself entangled with the IRS, frustrated by the lack of progress, or feels mistreated, involving us at any point can provide a fresh perspective and a strategic approach to resolve the situation. Whether preventing issues or addressing existing ones, we are here to guide businesses through the labyrinth of IRS complexities.

CHAPTER 4

INSTITUTIONAL INEFFICIENCY: THE IRS COLLECTIONS PROCESS

As mentioned earlier, the IRS can often be a source of frustration and anxiety for many individuals. It can feel like navigating a confusing maze, with various IRS divisions and notices that appear to operate independently and provide conflicting information. You might even wonder if the IRS intentionally complicates the process, and the truth is, it often does. Based on my experience, this complexity serves a deliberate purpose. It's designed to make it more convenient for individuals to opt for compliance and payment rather than enduring long wait times and receiving inconsistent guidance. This approach is cost-effective for the IRS, as it's a more efficient alternative to handling each case individually with a Revenue Officer. Understanding this concept can help alleviate some of the frustration, as you'll recognize the reasons behind this seemingly inefficient process.

Navigating IRS Notices: Essential Actions For Businesses

The IRS collections process typically unfolds over about three years before the IRS intensifies its efforts. While there are instances where the IRS acts swiftly, most of the time, you'll receive a series of notices before they escalate the case. These notices can range from gentle reminders to persistent letters, eventually culminating in certified letters. As such, it's imperative to take a proactive approach to handling these notices. In some cases, business owners entrust this responsibility to their bookkeepers or CPAs, which can lead to complications if the notices are disregarded and accumulate over time.

Ultimately, the responsibility for staying informed falls squarely on the business owner. Be sure to personally open your mail and monitor your bank accounts to spot any IRS actions. This isn't about a lack of trust in your CPA; it's just that the IRS is indifferent to who you may have appointed to handle your affairs. They see it as your duty to stay informed about your tax situation. Once you identify issues, take immediate action to address the underlying problems and collaborate with the IRS to resolve them.

The Consequences Of Ignoring IRS Collection Efforts

Procrastination in responding to IRS collection efforts can have far-reaching negative consequences for businesses. In most cases, business owners are aware of their tax obligations but tend to prioritize other expenses, such as employee payroll, over tax payments. While this approach may work for a while, it's essential to recognize that tax penalties can quickly accumulate, creating a substantial burden. What's more, failing to address these issues can lead to severe consequences, particularly for businesses reliant on government funding, such as healthcare providers, as the government has the authority to withhold payments. If this happens, it can stop the business operations in its tracks.

To mitigate these issues, it's vital to have a proactive plan in place to prevent recurring tax payment problems. This may involve establishing financial safeguards, securing a credit line, or creating a reserve fund. At the end of the day, proactive problem-solving is key. However, if you find yourself in a situation where your employees can't be paid due to tax issues, seeking professional assistance immediately is crucial to navigating the complexities of resolving the situation.

The Do's & Don'ts Of Navigating IRS Collections

I've encountered a couple of situations that provide excellent examples of the "do's and don'ts" when it comes to dealing with the IRS collections process...

Don't *Ignore The Situation & Try To Talk Your Way Out Of It*

I once had a client who ran an aviation business with multiple entities. Over the course of time, he received a series of IRS notices - but chose to ignore or procrastinate in addressing them. This ultimately led to a criminal investigation officer showing up at his doorstep to schedule a meeting.

He believed he could simply explain his situation and resolve things without professional representation by making statements highlighting actions that were against both federal laws and IRS regulations.

Do *Contact An Attorney At Once & Get On The Road To Resolution*

In contrast, consider the case of a landscaping business owner I've worked with, who owed millions in payroll taxes. Every time he received an IRS notice, he promptly shared it with me and sought guidance on how to deal with it. At times, I offered pragmatic advice on how he could take action directly and efficiently. At other times, I advised him not to handle certain matters himself, and I personally managed his liabilities in a strategic manner.

As a result, his business continues to operate today, he's on track to save approximately $4 million when the collection statute expires, and the IRS is content with the steps we've taken to address the situation. The key takeaway? Being professional, pragmatic, and expecting diligence both from yourself and the IRS can be highly beneficial.

Chapter 5

The Truth Will Set You Free: Navigating Financial Production & Analysis

I firmly believe that the saying "the truth will set you free" perfectly encapsulates the importance of accurate financial production when dealing with the IRS. Whenever I work with clients facing IRS issues, I emphasize the need for transparency. I tell them, "Give me everything." It's crucial not to hide any financial details. Whether you have a Maserati in the garage or other assets, I need to know about them so that I can protect your interests effectively.

In numerous instances, when a client employs both a bookkeeper and a CPA, their financial information tends to be well-organized. However, there are times when family members, such as an ex-spouse or a daughter who is studying accounting, take charge of managing the books. As you can imagine, this type of situation can easily result in a more complicated case review. Regardless of who is responsible for bookkeeping, it is imperative that the business owner conducts a meticulous review of the financial records. It's not uncommon for owners to think about hiding specific information, either under the assumption that it's irrelevant or out of fear that it might provoke additional demands from the IRS.

But here's the key: *Honesty is paramount.* Sharing all relevant financial information allows me to represent you better. The financial production serves as a critical negotiation tool, offering insights into the business's financial health, its liabilities, expenses, and overall financial landscape. When I have all the necessary information at hand, we can negotiate more effectively. There have been instances where a client's financial statement suggested they could pay the IRS $50,000 per month, but a closer look at their bank statements revealed a different reality. Remember: To avoid delays and to achieve a fair outcome in negotiations, every possible discrepancy needs to be addressed and resolved.

I've been caught by surprise far too many times when undisclosed assets suddenly emerge in the financial picture. It could be a boat, real estate, or other possessions that the client never mentioned. Regardless of what it is, when the IRS uncovers such assets, it can create problems because it will appear as though you were intentionally hiding information.

For example, I recall one memorable case where a client, who owned a horse stable, failed to disclose several horses registered under the business's name that had been purchased as a gift for his daughter. The IRS discovered them and was pushing for their sale. Unsurprisingly, a heated conversation ensued between myself, the client, and the Revenue

Officer. By the time the call was over, my client was so upset that he was threatening to harm the horses just to gain control of the situation. Thankfully, that didn't happen, and we managed to find a solution that both allowed him to keep his daughter's horses and restructure the negotiation.

Of course, not every situation escalates to the level of intensity as the one in this example, but it's quite common for personal and business assets to become a contentious matter. This is yet another reason why having a professional by your side who can evaluate the situation from a broader perspective is beneficial for both the client and the IRS. Our objective is to secure the best possible resolution - and sometimes that means stepping back from emotionally charged situations and directing our attention to the facts.

Regular Financial Analysis Is Paramount

In the context of IRS matters, it's always a good idea to be aware of your financial risks and find ways to trim your tax bill. While having a CPA or bookkeeper helps you keep track of your income and expenses, it's equally important to conduct an annual analysis of your profit and loss and carefully review your bank statements. In part, this is because finding an issue after just one quarter of imbalances is much easier to address and fix than waiting for three years of problems to pile up. That's why we strongly encourage staying on top of your finances and making plans to minimize your tax liabilities. The alternative, paying penalties due to late filings, like your 941, as they continue to compound is like throwing salt in the ocean.

Of course, there are times when people just aren't aware of these issues. In fact, I once had a client facing $30,000 in penalties for late filing of their income tax returns. Their CPA had all the necessary documents, but just didn't submit them on time and rolled the late filing penalties into the total balance due. The client wasn't foolish to trust their CPA, but they could have easily identified the issue by performing a more thorough personal review.

The conclusion here is that it's crucial to keep track of your financial situation. If you ever find yourself in trouble, having accurate profit and loss statements or well-maintained books makes the process much more efficient and cost-effective. It saves us from needing to extend deadlines, file appeals, or postpone timeframes just because we couldn't get the financial records in order. Often, a big portion of our work at Complex Tax Law Division involves just that – holding off the IRS while we work out the company's financial standing to determine what can be paid. Meanwhile, proactively preventing these issues by getting ahead of them and operating your business with either a quarterly or bi-quarterly bookkeeping system can be extremely beneficial and save you substantial amounts of time, effort, money, and headaches later down the road.

CHAPTER 6

HELP ME HELP YOU: AGREEMENTS & OFFERS

In my line of work, I often come across clients who are eager to explore the possibility of resolving their tax issues with the IRS. They've heard stories about programs like the Fresh Start program or settling their debts for pennies on the dollar. It's natural to want to save money, but it's crucial to understand that the IRS is primarily focused on collecting taxes, not settling them. So, when clients ask me about settling with the IRS, I often say, "*Help me help you.*"

The reality is that not everyone qualifies for an *Offer in Compromise,* which is essentially the IRS's version of a "settlement." To be eligible for this, the IRS needs to believe that they won't be able to collect the full amount you owe. In many cases, pursuing an Offer In Compromise might end up costing you more than a more pragmatic, long-term agreement. So, it's essential to be cautious about buying into the idea of quick, money-saving solutions, keeping in mind that the IRS's penalties and interest rates can be incredibly high and are non-negotiable.

Navigating IRS Negotiations For Long-Term Solutions

In our negotiations, we aim to structure agreements that allow businesses to continue their operations while potentially paying less than the total amount owed. The penalties and interest components of IRS debt can be brutal, and they're not something you can easily get rid of. However, with careful negotiation and a focus on your business's financial health, we can create agreements that help you navigate rough times while ensuring that your tax liabilities don't become overwhelming.

Fortunately, the IRS offers a wide variety of agreements that can be tailored to different business situations - but they don't always publicize these options. For instance, in my practice in Colorado, I've worked with clients in the cannabis industry who experience significant fluctuations in their income due to grow seasons. Similar challenges arise for those in the farming industry. In these cases, the IRS can establish what are known as cyclical agreements, where tax payments vary based on the season. This flexibility allows these businesses to stay compliant with their tax obligations, even with fluctuating incomes.

Taking this example to another industry, you might note that contractors dealing with retention accounts face another unique set of challenges. The funds they hold may not be readily available for paying off IRS debts because they're earmarked for specific projects. In such cases, we can negotiate graduated agreements that align with their cash flow, ensuring they can meet their tax obligations when they receive payment on their contracts.

The key takeaway is that there are numerous ways to structure agreements with the IRS, and the IRS doesn't always reveal these options readily. That's where a tax attorney or negotiator like myself comes in handy. We can navigate the complexities of IRS negotiations, ensuring that your business can continue its operations while addressing its tax liabilities.

The Consequences Of Defaulting On An IRS Agreement

Defaulting on an IRS agreement is never a favorable outcome. We put considerable effort into securing these agreements, and it's disheartening when clients find themselves in a situation where they can't or won't fulfill they're end of the deal. Naturally, defaults can happen for various reasons, including additional assessments, missed payments, or increased tax liabilities. Regardless, it's worth noting that the consequences of default can vary depending on your history with the IRS.

If it's a first-time default, it may be relatively easy to correct through an appeal and reinstatement process. However, if you have a history of defaults, things become much more complicated. The IRS doesn't want to be an ongoing partner in a failing business, and if your business repeatedly defaults, they may take actions to promote closure. In such cases, it becomes essential to strategize and make significant changes to your business operations to demonstrate to the IRS that you're committed to compliance. While some clients may find themselves in a cycle of renegotiating agreements each year, our goal is to prevent this from happening by helping them address the root causes of their tax issues.

The Role Of Financial Analysis & Documentation In Negotiating IRS Agreements

Financial analysis and proper documentation play a critical role in the negotiation and finalization of agreements with the IRS. Your financial records are like the key to a treasure chest during these negotiations, providing the necessary information to support your proposed terms and demonstrate your ability to meet your tax obligations. When we submit this financial information to the IRS, they scrutinize it carefully. If they disagree with any part of our proposal, they will communicate their concerns, opening the door to further negotiation or even an appeal. If it wasn't available before, this is where having accurate and well-documented financial information becomes absolutely crucial.

Another big advantage of conducting financial analysis is that if the IRS disagrees with your proposal, they have to respond before taking any harsh actions like levies or seizures. In simple terms, they must either agree or disagree. When the IRS disagrees with your proposal, it kicks off an appeals process, and your case is passed to a third-party appeals division. The advantage comes in the way that, from my experience, these Appeals Officers tend to be more down-to-earth and professional, often leading to more favorable outcomes for our clients.

Real-World Example: Transportation Company Suffered... Until Appeals Helped Them

A real-world example of the impact of financial analysis involves a transportation company that I represented. They operate buses shuttling passengers from hotels to airports, and it's quite an extensive fleet, with around 50 different vehicles, each having unique VINs and various loans. Unfortunately, the operation's financials weren't in the best shape, which led to tax issues with the IRS.

The Revenue Officer assigned to their case was incredibly diligent, almost to the point of obsession. They meticulously scrutinized each individual vehicle, VIN, and loan amount, trying to make sense of how it all connected to the company. But this led to major problems, as these buses were constantly in and out of service, frequently traded, and had various loans, making it all incredibly challenging to track.

This Revenue Officer kept rejecting our proposals time and again because we couldn't provide all the VINs and make everything align perfectly. It was a frustrating ordeal that lasted for six months – until I finally decided to file an appeal after numerous rejections. I secured a hearing with an Appeals Officer who reviewed the case's history and simply said, "I don't understand why the Revenue Officer is fixated on these details. It's evident that this is a transportation company, and here's what they can realistically pay. Let's establish an agreement."

After navigating through the frustration with the Revenue Officer and the exhaustive production of VINs, the Appeals Officer looked at the situation from a more practical financial perspective. They decided to stop the fuss and instead focus on setting up a payment plan to address the debt.

Naturally, this resolution was a game-changer for the client, who had been on the verge of closing their business, feeling like there was no way out of the IRS's grip. Thanks to the appeals process and the ability to showcase the financial realities, they managed to find a solution that worked, and they've been compliant ever since. Needless to say, it was a tremendous relief for the client to get past the roadblocks and work with someone who could genuinely understand and resolve the case.

In conclusion, financial analysis and documentation are the cornerstones of successful negotiations with the IRS. They enable us to present a clear and compelling case, increasing the likelihood of finding a resolution that works for both the IRS and our clients.

CHAPTER 7

THAT JUST GOT SPICY: LEVIES, SEIZURES, & GARNISHMENTS

Being from Colorado, I'm both a mountaineer and a rock climber. The term "that just got spicy" hails from British rock-climbing lore, possibly from Edmund Hillary or someone like Mallory. They used it on Everest when they found themselves in the death zone, when they were running out of oxygen, when there were blizzards closing in, or when they lost a crampon. In classic British humor, they remarked, "Well, that just got a little spicy up there." I always found that endearing, highlighting the understated humor the British have even in the face of significant and impactful situations.

To me, the things that "get a little spicy" in IRS collections are when the IRS has exhausted their last notice requirement without receiving what they needed or even hearing from the taxpayer. If they have heard from the taxpayer, it means the taxpayer hasn't complied with their requests. In such cases, the IRS can take drastic actions - emptying bank accounts, seizing assets, garnishing wages, and sending levies to accounts receivable.

This can be particularly harmful to a company relying on accounts receivable. Not only can they lose the funds from these accounts, but those accounts may also sever ties. These are the critical issues in IRS collections for businesses that we work tirelessly to prevent. If a client does come to us with active levies, garnishments, or a seizure in progress, that's when we muster all hands on deck to save the company from closure, ensure employee payroll is met, and protect innocent parties from harm.

The Timeline Leading Up To An IRS Levy Or Seizure

It can take the IRS up to three years before they send out the first notices for a levy, seizure, or garnishment. Typically, there's a significant lead-up to a levy action, however, there are exceptions to this rule. Recently, we had a client where we'd submitted all the necessary financial documents and proposals, following the standard negotiation process. Surprisingly, a Revenue Officer jumped the gun without checking for existing files or a power of attorney, issuing several levies. The client realized this when he tried to use his debit card and found it empty. This was a concerning situation, not just for him but also for me, as it implied a lack of proper representation.

We engaged in a professional yet heated conversation with the Revenue Officer. Subsequently, I had a follow-up conversation with his manager. Thankfully, they immediately released the levy and offered an apology. This incident emphasized the importance of having professional representation. However, it's crucial to note that there are steps to prevent situations like this from arising.

Before a levy is issued, there are several notices sent out. The first notice can be paid, the second allows for discussions on payment arrangements, and the third, the final notice, can be appealed to avoid a levy. After the appeals process, there's the final notice section. By responding promptly, filing taxes, and paying current taxes, negotiations with the IRS are possible. However, the Achilles' heel of any installment agreement or negotiation is continued tax accrual. If you fail to file or pay current taxes, the IRS is legally barred from setting up an agreement. Revenue Officers are then obligated to move forward with levies, even if they don't want to, as they view your business as failing.

Tax Relief Programs And Options For Businesses To Negotiate An Installment Agreement Or Other Resolution Through The IRS

In this industry, I've learned that the IRS and state agencies can sometimes act vindictively or irrationally. Here's a story to illustrate my point. We had negotiated a payment arrangement with a client, and everything had been submitted to the state agent for approval. We were awaiting their response, when unbeknownst to the client, their payroll company failed to file a return at the end of the year, intending to do it after the holiday season.

On New Year's Eve, I received a call from the client in a rather alarming situation. The state agent had shown up at the local bank and emptied their entire payroll account, which amounted to several hundred thousand dollars. This was done without any prior contact with me or the client. It was New Year's Eve, and banks were closed all weekend. The client's payroll for the holiday season had vanished. I found myself berating the state agent on my cell phone while watching a soccer game at a bar. Eventually, after considerable effort, I managed to get most of the money returned, but this incident taught me never to assume that the IRS or state agencies will be accommodating, even if they claim to be. Lesson learned. You must take charge of your own affairs, ensure proper filings, and follow your counsel's advice to avoid such situations involving levies and seizures.

CHAPTER 8

A SECOND BITE AT THE APPLE: THE POWER OF APPEALS

Appeals are a priceless asset in our negotiation arsenal. It never ceases to amaze me that representatives don't use Appeals as often as they could, given that it's a fundamental right for taxpayers. Some of my colleagues, not necessarily attorneys, have questioned why I file so many Appeals. My response has always been that it's our responsibility to advocate for the taxpayer's rights in their best interests, and that's precisely what Appeals allow us to do. This is why we often refer to Appeals as a "second bite at the apple" because they provide an opportunity to challenge various IRS decisions, including levies, audits, or rejected installment agreements.

Appeals offer a fresh perspective, especially when it seems like a Revenue Officer or someone on the other end of the phone isn't dedicating the necessary time to comprehend the financial intricacies of your case. We consider Appeals a crucial tool and particularly appreciate Appeals Hearings because we know we're interacting with professionals who approach cases with a practical mindset. More often than not, this approach leads to solutions that benefit all parties involved and that are aligned with our client's best interests.

When To Consider An IRS Appeal And Compliance Matters

I hold Appeals in high regard, but there's one crucial condition – staying on top of your current tax payments. To be eligible for an Appeal for back taxes owed, it's essential that your company remains up-to-date with its taxes currently. It has to stop the bleeding before it can bandage the wound - so to speak. This is the key requirement. For example, if your company owes back 941 liabilities and you're struggling to meet your current payroll taxes, you might be wondering, "Can I Appeal this?" Unfortunately, the answer is no. The first step is to catch up on your current payments, file your current returns, and settle your current taxes as a priority. Often, the conversation centers around achieving compliance with what you owe now and moving forward before we can start the Appeal Process for prior years and periods of taxes incurred.

Furthermore, it's crucial to remain compliant throughout the Appeal Process. If, for instance, you're not in compliance when the Appeal hearing arrives, there won't even be a chance to discuss your case; it will be dismissed due to this technicality. Aside from this compliance requirement, there are very few situations where you can't Appeal an IRS decision. If the IRS has turned down a proposal or suggested an action you disagree with, there are various types of Appeals available, each with its own pros and cons.

These Appeals align with your rights as a taxpayer, giving you the power to challenge decisions when you believe they are incorrect or unfair.

Different Types Of Appeals And Strategies

Selecting the right type of Appeal strategy hinges on the unique circumstances of your case, so it's highly advisable to seek counsel from a tax attorney. Remember: The IRS's website or internal revenue manual might not provide all the answers you need and the different types of Appeals available to you vary depending on your situation.

For instance, there's the Collection Due Process Appeal to halt issuance of levies, Equivalent Hearings for missed appeals deadlines, and Collection Appeal Processes for errantly filed Liens, Garnishments or erroneous actions taken by the IRS. In some cases, I've managed situations where I filed multiple Appeals simultaneously, withdrawing all others as soon as the first Appeal was acknowledged. This tactical approach streamlined my client's path to resolution.

At the end of the day, when it comes to Appeals, there's a great opportunity for creative problem-solving and thinking outside the box. With all that said, I strongly discourage filing an Appeal without professional representation. While there may be isolated instances of success for those who go it alone, more often than not, having expert guidance is in your best interest.

Potential Outcomes Of IRS Appeals For Businesses

Losing an Appeal isn't the end of the world. It's crucial to understand that an unsuccessful Appeal doesn't immediately result in property seizures, levies, or finalizing an audit. In most cases, the matter simply reverts to the collections stage. However, there are exceptions, like in offer and compromise cases, where a lost Appeal can mean you won't be granted an offer. Even still, you'll retain the chance to re-engage in negotiations with collections.

The real value of Appeals lies in their potential for successful resolutions. For example, an Appeals

Officer can remove bank account attachments initiated by a Revenue Officer. After a successful Appeal, the Appeals Officer can instruct the Revenue Officer to release the levies. This highlights why the benefits of filing an Appeal outweigh any potential drawbacks. It provides an additional opportunity to address your case thoughtfully and reach an effective resolution.

CHAPTER 9

KID GLOVES: HANDLING TAX LIENS WITH CARE

When it comes to discussions about Tax Liens, especially with underwriters, brokers, and title agents, I've learned to tread lightly. This isn't a reflection on my friends in the lending agencies but, the truth is, handling these conversations requires kid gloves, and an approach that is both patient and nuanced.

Often, when closing on a business or real estate loan, multiple parties at a title company and underwriting scrutinize the deal at the last minute. They might suddenly discover a Tax Lien and panic, wondering when it will be resolved. The irony is that I might have discussed the same matter with these very same parties five weeks prior, assuring them that it was resolved. Yet, I find myself re-explaining the logistics, drafting letters, and presenting IRS documentation to ease their concerns.

Fortunately, we've established what we call a "lien unit" within our firm for precisely this purpose. We've found it essential to provide this service to our clients as, in many cases, clients have already paid off the liens, but they still appear on old title reports. This discrepancy often leads to confusion and requires us to explain to title companies that the lien has indeed been cleared and paid, and it's no longer recorded with the IRS. As such, we must provide IRS documentation and clarify how these liens apply. Of course, the numbers don't always align, which adds to the complexity of the explanation, but the ultimate goal is to verify that the lien won't hinder the loan issuance.

There are three possible outcomes when addressing Tax Liens: discharge, release, or subordination:

- **Discharge** is the simplest, where the IRS will not encumber the asset used as collateral for the loan.
- **Release** means the lien has been entirely removed.
- **Subordination** is more intricate; it involves placing the lien in second position, ensuring the lender retains the primary claim over the assets being encumbered by the loan.

Naturally, these processes take time, and having an attorney experienced in this area, who understands the necessary documentation and timeframes, is invaluable. You have to keep in mind, these matters don't require just one explanation; it's an explanation for the broker, title, underwriting, underwriting's legal team, and possibly multiple rounds to facilitate it.

Once completed, it's crucial to verify that the funds go to the correct recipients for the liens to be genuinely released. This process is complex but serves all parties involved - ensuring correct procedures for the title are followed, protecting underwriters with legal documentation, and enabling clients and brokers alike to secure funding vital for their business operations or tax payments.

Additional Insights Before Moving Forward

One anecdotal point to note, especially regarding subordination, is that some lenders might seek to encumber your accounts receivable. (This frequently happens with factoring companies.) When this happens, subordination needs to be reestablished every 90 days. If a factoring company wants to secure a loan and requests a discharge of the lien on accounts receivable for a business that's generating consistent income, they should be aware that subordination is a quarterly affair.

As long as this is understood, it can benefit both the client and the factoring company. However, there have been cases where this wasn't communicated effectively, leading to IRS account receivable levies and repayment issues for the lending institution. It's crucial for lenders to comprehend the nature of the loan and the scope of the discharge being secured. A tax attorney can play a pivotal role in ensuring a smooth process in such cases.

CHAPTER 10

THE BUCK STOPS WITH YOU: THE TRUTH ABOUT TRUST FUND ASSESSMENTS

When it comes to tax responsibilities, the old saying holds true: *The buck stops with you.* As the business owner, you're ultimately responsible for ensuring your employees' payroll taxes are properly handled. So while it's not uncommon to hear stories about others being involved in tax-related tasks, such as an ex-spouse managing the books or a CPA mishandling employment tax returns (941s), the IRS doesn't let anyone off the hook easily.

At the end of the day, it's the business owner's neck on the line, and in some cases, even a third party like a bookkeeper who was aware of the issues can be held liable. What's more, the IRS doesn't hold employees accountable for payroll taxes. So, if taxes were withheld from an employee's paycheck but not sent to the IRS, it's the business owner who faces the consequences. This can lead to significant liabilities and serious personal repercussions. The IRS views this lack of payment as theft and fraud, and these situations trigger a *trust fund assessment.*

Trust fund assessments can be substantial, and it's essential to address them promptly. I'll share a couple of examples to illustrate how these assessments can play out and how to handle them effectively.

The Trust Fund Recovery Penalty For Employment Taxes

Here, I'll share both a cautionary tale and a success story to demonstrate the do's and don'ts of handling trust fund assessments…

The Cautionary Tale: A Business Owner Who Pointed Fingers & Ran Away

Years ago, I was called in to represent a staffing company. In a situation that's quite common in the staffing industry, this company didn't have many physical assets; it was all about lending employees to other businesses. This particular staffing company was providing employees to a major computer company, and there was a significant amount of money changing hands. Unfortunately, the person in charge lost control of the taxes and, in the end, there were millions and millions of dollars in trust fund assessments.

In the face of this, the individual behind the staffing company was reluctant to take any action on their own behalf. It became a tangled mess of finger-pointing – this person didn't file that return, that person didn't pay this money, and so on. At some point, I had to have a frank conversation with the owner. I explained that it didn't matter whose fault it was. The assessments were in their name because they were listed as the owner of the company. The taxes were owed.

However, they persisted in claiming that they didn't owe the money, and the IRS pursued the matter to the extent that they decided to leave the country. Naturally, this forced me to discontinue my representation because I don't handle cases involving individuals engaged in international tax avoidance. From my perspective, this ending demonstrates just about the worst-case scenario.

The Success Story: A Partnership Who Took Responsibility & Came Out On Top

Now, let me share a positive example of how to handle a trust fund assessment. My client operated a medical health company that had individuals in their nursing homes who didn't actually qualify for medical aid. As a result, they had unpaid balances because the government didn't reimburse them for the services they provided. Once again, we were looking at millions of dollars in trust fund assessments.

However, in this case, the two individuals involved were quite forthright about the situation. So, after some time and some substantial negotiation, we managed to arrange monthly payments of around $500 for the millions they owed. The IRS recognized that it was a case of a failed business and was willing to work with them. And my clients? They understood that the aim of the IRS wasn't to bankrupt them, but to ensure they made an honest effort to deal with the situation even if full payment of the debt would never be a possibility.

Of course, it's not an ideal situation when the IRS is pursuing you for trust fund assessments due to theft and fraud. However, there are steps that can be taken to either delay these assessments so they can be paid, or once they are assessed, to protect your income and assets as an officer. The goal is to enable you to continue your life without being burdened by crippling debts - or facing the prospect of being criminally charged and prosecuted for international tax avoidance.

CHAPTER 11

PUTTING LIPSTICK ON A PIG: SUCCESSOR & ALTER EGO DETERMINATIONS

In the context of tax liabilities, it's essential to grasp the concept of successorship and alter ego determinations. You can't just close down a company with substantial tax debts, establish a new company with a different Employer Identification Number (EIN), and continue business as usual. This approach is often seen as an attempt to evade tax responsibilities and it doesn't work. It's akin to putting lipstick on a pig

– while you may try to make it look otherwise, the core company remains unchanged.

The IRS takes a keen interest in cases where a company changes EINs but retains nearly identical operational elements, including the owner, equipment, clients, and more. In such cases, the IRS may label it as an alter ego or successor entity. This implies they can shift the outstanding tax balances from the old entity to the new one, along with penalties and interest. And in the worst instances, this move could even trigger a criminal investigation.

The Impact Of Successor & Alter Ego Determination On Your Tax Liability

The main purpose of creating separate business entities is to shield individuals from civil liabilities and, to some extent, taxation liabilities arising from business operations. However, these entities can't be misused to evade tax payments or obscure a business's tax obligations. So when the IRS identifies an alter ego or successor, it marks a significant development in the collections process.

If a Revenue Officer suspects that an entity might be an alter ego or successor, they must go through a legal process to confirm their suspicions, including a comprehensive review by the IRS legal department. If your business structure is legitimate, (for example, if it involves a parent company and its subsidiary), and the Revenue Officer is merely investigating for irregularities, a tax attorney can help clarify the situation and prove that there is no alter ego or successor relationship.

However, addressing this matter aggressively and proactively is crucial because the determination process often happens discreetly. If a Revenue Officer informs you or your CPA that they are looking into successorship, it's advisable to involve a tax attorney immediately to ensure you can mount a strong defense if there are valid reasons to do so.

When Legal Protections & Tax Liabilities Can Be Transferred To A Successor Company

In cases where a company must close and there are outstanding tax liabilities, creative solutions may be necessary to avoid alter ego or successor determinations. For instance, if a business closes because of state unemployment tax issues unrelated to its federal tax obligations, a new entity cannot be formed to sidestep the tax liabilities, as this would result in an alter ego determination.

Instead, a viable approach, which should be discussed with the assigned Revenue Officer, involves creating a new entity while maintaining an installment agreement for the old entity's debt. This arrangement can be structured as a third-party assignee agreement. By doing this, you demonstrate to the IRS that you're not trying to evade taxes but are merely seeking a practical solution to your financial problems. Of course, proper documentation and a cooperative relationship with the IRS are essential for success in such cases.

This strategy allows the new entity to move forward without the burden of the old entity's Tax Lien, making it easier to secure loans or financing. It's a win-win situation, as the IRS continues to receive payments, and you can continue your business activities without unnecessary impediments.

The Role Of Due Diligence In Determining An Alter Ego

The IRS typically looks for specific indicators when assessing whether an entity is an alter ego or successor. These indicators include similarities in assets, clientele, naming conventions, bank accounts, and phone numbers. The most straightforward case for the IRS to identify is when a new EIN is used, but the rest of the operation remains nearly identical.

However, if there is a legitimate transfer of assets between two completely separate entities, that is a different situation. For example, if one LLC purchases a struggling company, and there is no intent to evade taxes, this is not considered an alter ego relationship. The key is to maintain two genuinely separate entities with distinct operations, bank accounts, client bases, and branding.

The Alter Ego Doctrine And Personal Liability

If you attempt to hide behind another entity, thinking it will shield you from the trust fund assessments or other tax liabilities of the original entity, know that it just doesn't work. The tax obligations can flow through - and they will if you are found out. A rather amusing, eye-rolling example of this was a short-term client of mine who tried this approach…

This client's new alter ego business was actually located just one floor up in the same office building as his previous business. When a Revenue Officer arrived, asking for him, he claimed he wasn't the person they were looking for and asked the officer to return and find someone else. Of course, when I heard this story, I had to inform the client that I couldn't represent him anymore because providing false information to the IRS is illegal.

I'm not sure how that situation eventually played out, but telling a Revenue Officer that you're not the person they're looking for while you're sitting in your alter ego is, to put it lightly, not a recommended approach. In fact, it's just about the worst way to handle such a situation. If a business owner finds themselves in a scenario with an alter ego or successor assessment and they are an officer of the successor entity, they shouldn't try to hide it - they should accept that those balances will simply transfer across, and they will be subject to the same trust fund liabilities as before.

Preventative Measures To Avoid Alter Ego Determinations

To prevent alter ego or successor determinations and maintain a clear separation between corporate and personal assets and liabilities, several steps should be taken:

- When closing one entity and opening another, ensure that the two entities are entirely separate. Do not maintain shared bank accounts or phone numbers.
- File dissolution paperwork for the old entity.
- Close bank accounts associated with the old entity.

- Use different phone numbers and contact information for the new entity.
- Avoid any actions that might suggest a financial connection between the old and new entities.

Properly addressing these aspects can help you avoid alter ego or successor determinations and maintain a clean separation between corporate and personal assets and liabilities. If a successor entity is necessary, consult with a tax attorney to ensure that the process is carried out correctly and transparently, with all necessary documentation in place to demonstrate compliance with tax laws and regulations.

CHAPTER 12

TAP DANCING ON THE HEAD OF THE NEEDLE: NAVIGATING AUDITS & RECONSIDERATIONS

When I think about audits, I see them as a series of delicate maneuvers that you have to accomplish at the most precarious tipping point. *Why?* Because, unlike the presumption of "*innocent until proven guilty*" used by the criminal justice system, IRS auditors operate on a "*guilty until proven innocent*" basis. In essence, the process looks like this: The IRS reviews your return, identifies concerns, and demands that you prove their assessment wrong. At this point, the IRS holds all the cards. This means that the success of any negotiation hinges on meticulous execution - *much like the precision required to tap dance on the head of a needle.*

To start, it's important to engage with an audit proactively, rather than waiting until the last minute. This approach allows us to set the stage for a productive negotiation or determine if the audit is, in fact, valid. By doing so, we can avoid unnecessary disputes and penalties and work towards a favorable outcome.

Identifying Common Triggers For IRS Audits

The IRS seems to operate using a mysterious algorithm - similar to something like the supercomputer HAL from Stanley Kubrick's classic film *2001: A Space Odyssey*. While we can't comprehend the inner workings of this algorithm, seemingly random red flags tend to trigger audits. For instance, when a tax return appears illogical - showing substantial income with no expenses or vice versa - it's likely to trigger an audit.

While the exact triggers for an audit remain elusive, most experienced CPAs can spot potential issues and take steps to prevent them. Even still, when a tax return exhibits these conspicuous disparities and fails the "laugh test," an audit becomes a real possibility.

Navigating An IRS Audit: Initial Steps

Receiving an IRS audit notification can be daunting, but understanding the process and your options is crucial. There are two primary types of audits to be aware of.

- **The first type**, known as a CP 523 audit, involves responding to IRS determinations through letters. You can reply with documentation directly, enlist the help of your CPA, or engage a tax attorney to respond.
- **The second type of audit** is more comprehensive and resembles scenes from movies like *The Wolf of Wall Street.* Auditors schedule meetings to meticulously examine your financial records. In these cases, it's essential to ensure the auditor

stays within the audit's defined scope to prevent unnecessary expansions.

Auditors are constrained by the audit's scope, unless they decide to expand it. Protecting your financial privacy is one of your rights and auditors cannot delve into your personal documents without a valid reason. However, having a tax attorney guide you through the process can help assert your rights more effectively. And remember: While it may be tempting to confront auditors aggressively, professionalism usually yields more favorable results. Auditors are, after all, just doing their jobs, and maintaining a respectful tone can often lead to a smoother audit process.

Exploring Tax Audit Reconsideration

Tax audit reconsideration is essentially a second look at your audit after it's been completed. If you didn't respond to the initial audit notice or are dissatisfied with the results, you can request reconsideration. However, this process comes with a caveat. Where assessments have already been made, you may have to deal with liens or ongoing collection actions - and managing both the audit reconsideration and collections concurrently can be complex, requiring careful strategizing.

As a business tax attorney, my primary role in audits and reconsiderations is to ensure that the IRS follows its own rules and regulations, ensuring that everything proceeds smoothly and efficiently, with all parties following the necessary protocols. I don't prepare tax returns or directly defend them during audits; that's the role of CPAs. However, I work to support CPAs, providing them with legal backing and ensuring they have the information necessary for the audit. Then, if collection actions arise, I help my clients navigate assessments, balances, and penalties that may have been imposed as a result.

Preventing Future Audits

Once you've experienced an IRS audit, preventing another one becomes a priority. Most people learn valuable lessons from the challenging process, such as how timely and accurate tax filings are crucial for minimizing the risk of facing an audit in the first place. For this reason, hiring professionals to handle your financial records and tax returns can save you the time, money, and stress associated with the process. Additionally, addressing any issues identified during the audit and implementing necessary changes in your financial practices can help you avoid future audits. While no one wants to face a situation such as this, each audit that occurs provides a valuable roadmap for improving your financial record-keeping and tax compliance, helping you steer clear of audits in the future.

CHAPTER 13

KNOWLEDGE IS POWER: THE WORLD OF FORENSIC AUDITING

The title of this chapter itself speaks volumes. Forensic auditing may sound intricate, and indeed it is. Fortunately, this is exactly what tax attorneys, including myself and my capable staff, excel at – deciphering intricate financial documents and presenting a clear narrative for those who may not be familiar with complex financial matters. Of course, we're not CPAs, so our aim isn't to dig into adjusted gross income or alternative minimum tax. Instead, we scrutinize bank statements, track money flows, and question discrepancies between what's disclosed and what we see.

In essence, our role is to guide clients away from potential financial pitfalls. For example, we might come across a business claiming to spend $40,000 weekly on payroll, yet we see their payroll company disbursing $80,000 every two days. This incongruity naturally raises questions, such as "Where is this additional money coming from?" Often, we discover that our client has omitted crucial information, like undisclosed bank accounts, which should be reported to the IRS and can give the impression that they're intentionally withholding information.

All in all, our forensic examination of financial records involves identifying such issues, correcting errors, and, in nearly 99% of cases, ensuring that a business's financial records align with the owner's understanding.

The Triggers Of Forensic Auditing

Often, forensic audits revolve around tax liability and assessing how much a company can realistically pay the IRS for its outstanding tax debts. Our goal is to minimize the monthly payment arrangement imposed by the IRS. But while a business might have the capacity to pay more, we prefer such payments to be voluntary. Hence, we scrutinize financials to identify income sources, expense patterns, and any discrepancies.

For instance, we had a client whose business account revealed monthly charges of $600 for a Farmville game app - a detail he was entirely unaware of. This discovery prompted a more thorough audit, uncovering wasteful spending across the board. Such seemingly minor recurring expenses can, over time, significantly dent a business's finances. I often refer to this phenomenon as "rich poor people" - where substantial income flows in and out, but financial oversight is lacking. Recognizing these inefficiencies is often half the battle, shedding light on how money is being spent.

In the grand scheme of things, individual transactions like a thousand dollars in monthly bank charges might not immediately raise alarms. However, when you aggregate numerous similar transactions, it can result in substantial losses when the money could be put to better use, such as settling taxes or reinvesting in the business. At the end of the day, we aim to ensure that the companies we work with can meet their IRS payment commitment, even in the worst-case scenario. To do this, we perform a comprehensive financial review, which can lead to various eye-opening discoveries.

The Range Of Applications For Forensic Auditing

Our financial expertise extends far beyond tax-related matters; it finds application in various contexts...

Civil Litigation Cases

In litigation situations, we can request up to six years' worth of bank statements and other pertinent documents to submit to our auditing practices. However, in non-litigation due diligence scenarios, limitations may emerge if we don't have access to all the necessary paperwork. We make every effort to define these constraints, even still, third-party restrictions on information disclosure can pose challenges. It's a complex yet intriguing process, one that can offer substantial benefits to business owners or individuals with significant financial interests at stake.

Beyond Taxes: Family Law Cases

What's more, we can employ the same techniques in family law cases, especially when one party has control over significant assets and business accounts. The truth is, sorting through stacks of paperwork filled with intricate financial details isn't the specialty of divorce or family law attorneys, but it's where we truly shine.

In fact, this form of forensic auditing can sometimes feel like conducting a criminal investigation, revealing hidden truths, or substantiating a party's claims to their advantage. We have the ability to uncover financial irregularities, like when one spouse claims to earn $10,000 per month while secretly managing an account generating $60,000 monthly. And in cases like these, our reports shed light on sometimes shadowy financial complexities, making the work that we do indispensable.

CHAPTER 14

SOMETHING FISHY IS GOING ON: EXPERT TESTIMONY & PERSONAL EXPERIENCES

"*Something fishy is going on...*" These are the words that found their way into a judge's final opinion of a case where I provided expert testimony. At the end of this case, she not only quoted me, but also expressed her agreement with my hunch that, somewhere beneath the surface, there was something awry in the transactions between the parties involved. This mention in the judge's opinion marked a significant win for my client, leaving them immensely satisfied.

Providing expert testimony in the field of taxation presents an intriguing departure from the typical litigation battleground. Instead of the usual intellectual combat, I adopt a pragmatic approach. I lay out the facts and highlight what's missing or questionable, all without directly accusing the opposing party. In the end, it's about letting the documents speak for themselves.

I've said it before and I'll say it again, *the truth will set you free.* When we encounter inconsistencies or irregularities, our goal is not to assign blame. It's about addressing what doesn't align with the facts and numbers, a responsibility I hold in high regard. For this reason, judges often rely on my experience as a tax attorney, which I've earned through years of handling complex cases and working with a diverse range of clients. This trust in my character and expertise often saves me from the typical courtroom battles. Instead, I can concentrate on my strengths, which involve simplifying intricate financial information for practical use in any situation.

How an Experienced Business Tax Law Attorney Utilizes Expert Testimony

In my role as a business tax law attorney, experience carries significant weight. As Peyton Manning wisely stated, "You do something 10,000 times, and you'll be an expert at it." I've certainly been part of more negotiations than I can count over the years. While I won't claim to have seen it all, my extensive involvement has undeniably molded me into an expert in negotiations, particularly within the realm of tax law.

My expertise goes beyond negotiations; it encompasses the broader field of tax law. I specialize in ensuring businesses remain operational, safeguarding assets, and meeting payroll obligations. Clients depend on my ability to anticipate potential issues and navigate them before they become insurmountable challenges.

Being an expert in negotiations also means I can share my knowledge with other attorneys who may not have a deep understanding of tax law or with CPAs who prefer not to delve into the intricacies of IRS negotiations. I'm well-versed in deciphering complex tax reports, even when they resemble intricate puzzles. My track record of successfully unraveling these complexities benefits not only my clients but also my colleagues, ultimately leading to favorable resolutions for everyone involved.

Final Thoughts

I'd like to conclude this book with a personal story that holds a special place in my journey. The very first client I took on when I opened my own firm six years ago brought with him an incredibly difficult case with many intricate issues. When I reflect on it today, I think that the name of my firm, the Complex Tax Law Firm, likely owes some of its inspiration to him.

I vividly remember him saying, "Steve, I'm going to hire you for this. I know you don't have many clients yet, but I know you - and I trust you." On that day, he essentially handed me the keys to the Ferrari, so to speak. At the time, he had nearly $1 million in unpaid tax liabilities. None of them were very legitimate, and as I delved into the case, I found that the Revenue Officers had gone significantly off course. In fact, the feds had veered so far off the beaten path that I found myself needing to file a Freedom of Information Act request, submit several audit reconsideration requests, and collaborate with a Taxpayer Advocate to sort out separate assessments of hundreds of thousands of dollars between him and his wife when they had actually filed jointly. It was a monumental mess to untangle.

Occasionally, my client and I would chat over the phone, and he'd say, "One day, Steve, we're going to be sitting down at the Brown Palace in Denver, and you'll pick up the tab, and we'll raise a toast to our successful case - that is if I don't end up getting divorced because the IRS is garnishing my wife's wages over this." At the time, it felt like a distant dream. I never truly believed we'd reach that point. The situation was so tangled that I had to consult with a woman who had extensive experience deep within the IRS's processing systems to explain how these various assessments had become so distorted. Even for her, it took months to untangle the web the federal government had created.

Fast forward to just two months ago, I found myself at the Brown Palace with this client and his wife and we celebrated our victorious journey. Needless to say, they were overjoyed. We resolved everything, rectified all the Tax Liens, freed up their properties, and navigated through all the complexities and challenges. Later that evening, after his wife had retired to their hotel room for the night, he and I sat around contemplating how we could continue working together. Despite all the hurdles, we had an incredible time battling the IRS for six years, and the outcome was truly satisfying.

For a moment, he even considered filing his return late just so I could continue representing him. I advised against it, of course, but it was heartwarming and immensely rewarding to have not only done my job successfully but to have done it for my very first client, who I hope will remain a friend for life. Despite the difficulties we faced, having him there with me through thick and thin, and being able to use my decades of experience to secure that result, was incredibly meaningful. This, to me, is the essence of what it's all about.

Index

9

941 liabilities · 67

A

alter ego · 85
Appeals · 65
Auditors · 93

B

bookkeeper · 48

C

certified public accountant · 36
CPAs · 105
credit line · 42
cyclical agreements · 53

D

Discharge · 73
divorce cases · 20
documentation · 55

E

Employer Identification Number · 82
employment tax returns · 77
expert testimony · 103

F

first-time abatement · 25
Fresh Start · 51

G

Government Paperwork Elimination Act · 30

I

intellectual back flips · 16
IRS negotiations · 12

L

legitimate transfer · 86
litigation · 99

O

Offer in Compromise · 27

P

payroll-intensive business · 20

R

reasonable cause request · 25
Release · 73
retention accounts · 53
Revenue Officer · 66

S

Subordination · 73
successorship · 82

T

title company · 21
trust fund assessment · 77

U

underwriter · 21

NOTES

Made in United States
Troutdale, OR
10/01/2026

55039585R00069